Whispers of Dawn" Journey of Healing and Rediscovery

DERICK CHIBILU

Published by Books By Derick Chibilu, 2024.

Table of Contents

.... 1

Book Description: 3

Chapter 1: Echoes of Laughter 5

Chapter 2: The Weight of Silence 7

Chapter 3: Anchored in Prayer 9

Chapter 4: Fragile Steps Forward 11

Chapter 5: A Community of Comfort 13

Chapter 6: Grasping at Memories 15

Chapter 7: Whispers of Doubt 17

Chapter 8: The Language of Flowers 19

Chapter 9: A Hand to Hold 21

Chapter 10: Unexpected Laughter 23

Chapter 11: Footprints in the Sand 25

Chapter 12: Questions in the Starlight 27

Chapter 13: Glimmers of Forgiveness 29

Chapter 14: A Shared Symphony 31

Chapter 15: Unveiling Secrets 33

Chapter 16: The Crossroads of Choice 35

Chapter 17: Faith Under Fire 37

Chapter 18: Broken Pieces Mending 39

Chapter 19: Dancing in the Rain 41

Chapter 20: The Art of Letting Go 43

Chapter 21: A Mother's Love Endures 45

Chapter 22: Facing the Unknown 47

Chapter 23: A Leap of Faith 49

Chapter 24: The Promise of Dawn 51

Chapter 25: Love's Second Chorus 53

Chapter 26: Whispers of Forever 55

ABOUT THE AUTHOR 57

BOOKS BY MR. DERICK CHIBILU 59
Author Contact Information 61

"Whispers of Dawn"

Journey of Healing and Rediscovery
BY

DERICK CHIBILU

****

Published by Books by Derick Chibilu
12000 Sawmill Rd Suite 2213, The Woodlands,
TX, United States, Texas
Website: www.booksbyderikchibilu.com[1]
Email: Thecblogger4@gmail.com
Contact Number: +1 346-328-1110
Publication Date: 01/10/2024
Cover design by Dacisco Video and Media Production Team

The content within this book is presented "as is" without any form of warranty, whether express or implied. This includes, but is not limited to, implied warranties of merchantability, fitness for a particular purpose, or non-infringement. The author and publisher disclaim any responsibility for any damages, including special, indirect, consequential, or incidental damages, as well as those related to lost profits, loss of revenue, or loss of use, arising from or connected to the use of this book. The opinions expressed in this book are the author's own and do not necessarily represent the views of the publisher.

Publisher's Note:

"Welcome to "Whispers of Dawn" a poignant tapestry woven with faith, hope, and the enduring power of second chances.

For permission requests, please contact the publisher at the address provided above or you can visit our

www.booksbyderickchibilu.com.[2]

---

1. http://www.booksbyderikchibilu.com

2. http://www.booksbyderickchibilu.com.

Book Description:

"Whispers of Dawn" is a heartfelt narrative that explores the journey of Ethan Miller through the intricate layers of grief, faith, and the healing power of love. The book captures the essence of the human experience, portraying the protagonist's struggle with loss, the weight of silence, and the solace found in prayer.

Throughout the chapters, the narrative delves into the themes of community support, unexpected connections, and the resilience required for single parenthood. The titles of the chapters, such as "Anchored in Prayer," "A Community of Comfort," and "A Hand to Hold," reflect the emotional and spiritual aspects of Ethan's voyage toward healing.

The symbolism within the chapter titles, like "The Language of Flowers" and "Footprints in the Sand," adds depth to the narrative, offering readers a nuanced exploration of Ethan's emotional landscape. The book gracefully navigates moments of doubt and the fragility of moving forward, ultimately weaving a tapestry of hope, forgiveness, and the enduring strength found in love.

When Ethan Miller loses his wife Sarah in a tragic accident, his world crumbles. He's left adrift in a sea of grief, clinging to shattered memories and a faith that feels distant. But through the kindness of his community, unwavering prayers, and the gentle nudges of fate, Ethan embarks on a journey of healing and rediscovery. As he navigates the complexities of single parenthood, grapples with lingering doubt, and opens his heart to unexpected connections, Ethan learns that love truly has no end. "Whispers of Dawn" is a poignant tapestry woven with faith, hope, and the enduring power of second chances.

Chapter 1: Echoes of Laughter

The scent of lavender and freshly baked bread, once comforting hallmarks of their cozy home, now mocked Ethan with their cruel familiarity. Empty laughter echoed in the cavernous silence, bouncing off the sun-drenched walls where framed photos of Sarah, his beloved wife, beamed back at him with smiles that felt like a lifetime ago. It had been six months since the car accident, six months since the light in his life had been extinguished, leaving behind an agonizing darkness.

Ethan wandered aimlessly, his fingertips tracing the worn edges of photo frames. Each image was a portal to a past filled with shared dreams, whispered secrets, and the melody of Sarah's infectious laughter. He could almost hear it now, tinkling like wind chimes, a sound that used to chase away his worries and fill him with warmth. Now, it was a phantom melody, haunting him with its absence.

He sank onto the couch, Sarah's favorite throw blanket wrapped around him like a shield against the encroaching despair. He buried his face in the fabric, inhaling the faint traces of her perfume, a bittersweet reminder of her touch. Tears, long held back, finally spilled over, hot and silent, soaking into the plush fibers.

Suddenly, a small hand tugged at his sleeve. Ethan looked down to meet the wide, innocent eyes of his five-year-old daughter, Lily. Her blonde curls, a mirror image of Sarah's, were mussed from sleep, and her pajamas bore the remnants of chocolate syrup from a bedtime snack.

"Daddy, are you crying?" she asked, her voice laced with concern. Ethan pulled her close, burying his face in her hair. The familiar scent of baby shampoo and sunshine offered a fleeting solace. He choked back a sob, not wanting to burden his fragile daughter with his grief.

"Just missing Mommy, sweetheart," he managed, his voice thick with emotion.

Lily climbed onto his lap, her small arms wrapping around his neck. "Me too," she whispered, her voice barely above a sigh.

In that moment, amidst the suffocating sorrow, a spark of determination flickered within Ethan. He couldn't crumble. He had to be strong, for Lily, for Sarah's memory. He had to find a way to carry on, not just survive, but live, truly live, even if the laughter felt like a distant echo.

With a shaky breath, Ethan pulled away, wiping his tears. He met Lily's gaze, a ghost of a smile playing on his lips.

"Come on, sweetheart," he said, his voice rough but hopeful. "Let's make breakfast. Mommy wouldn't want us to be sad, would she?"

Lily's eyes brightened, a hint of her mother's smile returning. "No, she wouldn't," she echoed, her voice gaining strength.

Together, they rose, hand in hand, the echoes of laughter replaced by the promise of a new beginning, a journey of healing fueled by love and faith, guided by the whispers of dawn.

Chapter 2: The Weight of Silence

The mornings became a routine dance of muted grief and determined strength for Ethan and Lily. Breakfasts were prepared in a hushed kitchen that once echoed with shared laughter. The weight of Sarah's absence pressed heavily on their hearts, and the silence within the walls of their home was a constant reminder of the void left by her departure.

Ethan, with each passing day, found himself grappling with the emptiness, a vacuum that seemed to expand in the quiet moments when he was alone. Lily, too young to fully comprehend the permanence of her mother's absence, filled the void with innocent questions and drawings that adorned the refrigerator – colorful expressions of a child's attempt to make sense of a world now defined by silence.

As Ethan sat at the kitchen table, sipping his coffee, he couldn't escape the overwhelming silence. The tick of the clock became a rhythmic reminder of time's unyielding march forward, indifferent to his grief. The weight of unanswered questions lingered in the air, and doubts crept into the corners of his mind like shadows cast by an unseen force.

One evening, as dusk painted the sky in hues of pink and gold, Ethan found himself standing in front of the small home altar adorned with a picture of Sarah and a flickering candle. The flame danced, casting dancing shadows on the photograph, and for a moment, it seemed as if Sarah's eyes held a secret, a message yet to be deciphered.

The weight of silence hung heavy in the room, and Ethan, guided by an inexplicable impulse, began to speak. Words, long held back, spilled forth as he recounted his day, his struggles, and the moments when he felt Sarah's presence most acutely. It was a conversation with the ether, a soliloquy of a grieving heart yearning for understanding.

In the quiet aftermath, as if in response to his unspoken plea, a soft breeze stirred the room, carrying with it the fragrance of blooming flowers. Ethan felt a gentle warmth enveloping him, a reassurance that love endured beyond the tangible. The weight of silence began to lift, replaced by a sense of connection that transcended the boundaries of the seen and unseen.

With newfound resolve, Ethan embraced the challenges of single parenthood with grace, knowing that the weight of silence could be transformed into a symphony of memories and shared love. The journey ahead was uncertain, but guided by faith, love, and the echoes of shared laughter, he pressed forward, eager to discover what the whispers of dawn held for him and Lily.

And so, the pages of their story turned, each chapter unveiling a tapestry woven with the threads of healing, hope, and the enduring power of a love that reached beyond the silence.

Chapter 3: Anchored in Prayer

The passage of time brought a subtle transformation to Ethan and Lily's home. With each sunrise, Ethan found solace in the routine of anchoring their days in prayer. The echoes of laughter that once resonated within the walls began to harmonize with whispered conversations with the divine, a source of strength and guidance.

As Ethan knelt by the bedside each morning, Lily would often join him, her innocent voice blending with his in a duet of heartfelt petitions. The act of prayer became a sacred ritual, a tether grounding them amidst the unpredictable waves of grief. The language of faith became their shared dialect, a means of communication that transcended spoken words.

In those moments of quiet reflection, Ethan discovered a reservoir of inner strength he hadn't known existed. The weight of responsibility as a single parent began to shift, buoyed by the unwavering support he felt from a source beyond the tangible. The whispers of dawn transformed into a chorus of hope, a symphony of assurance that they were not navigating this journey alone.

One evening, as dusk bathed their home in a warm glow, Ethan and Lily sat together on the porch. The rhythmic cadence of their prayers lingered in the air, creating an atmosphere of peace. Lily, with her wide eyes full of wonder, looked up at the darkening sky.

"Daddy," she began, her voice soft, "do you think Mommy hears us when we pray?"

Ethan smiled, a mixture of sadness and reassurance. "I believe she does, sweetheart. Our prayers are like whispers that reach her wherever she is. She may not be here with us, but she's always a part of our hearts."

Lily nodded, seemingly comforted by the thought. The evening breeze carried with it a sense of communion, as if their prayers were woven into the fabric of the universe, creating a connection that transcended the boundaries of time and space.

In the days that followed, Ethan and Lily continued their prayerful journey, finding strength in the moments of silence, and solace in the belief that love, in its purest form, could bridge the gap between the seen and the unseen.

An unexpected sense of peace settled within Ethan, a peace that surpassed the understanding of those who observed their journey from the outside. The weight of silence, once an oppressive force, became a tapestry adorned with threads of faith and anchored in the belief that, even in the midst of loss, the echoes of laughter and the whispers of dawn could guide them toward a brighter tomorrow.

Chapter 4: Fragile Steps Forward

Days turned into weeks, and the rhythm of prayer continued to weave its way through the fabric of Ethan and Lily's lives. The fragrance of freshly baked bread and the comforting scent of lavender no longer taunted Ethan but became familiar companions, marking the passage of time in their journey of healing.

In the midst of the routine, small moments of grace began to emerge. Lily, with her resilient spirit, brought laughter back into their home. Her giggles echoed through the halls, a testament to the resilience of a child's heart, finding joy amidst the shadows of sorrow.

One sunny afternoon, as Ethan tended to the garden, Lily, armed with a plastic shovel and a determined expression, joined him. The vibrant colors of blooming flowers mirrored the hope that blossomed within their hearts. With each delicate petal and leaf, they nurtured not only the garden but also the fragile seeds of resilience that sprouted within their souls.

As they knelt in the soil, hands dirty but hearts light, Ethan couldn't help but marvel at the simple beauty of the moment. Lily's laughter, a melody that resonated with newfound joy, mingled with the rustle of leaves and the distant hum of the neighborhood. It was a symphony of life, a reminder that even in the wake of loss, life continued to bloom.

In the evenings, Ethan and Lily would take walks around their neighborhood. The whispers of dawn transformed into the golden glow of sunset, casting long shadows on the pavement. Each step forward felt like a triumph over the weight of silence, a testament to their resilience and the enduring power of love.

One evening, as they walked hand in hand, Lily spoke up, breaking the comfortable silence. "Daddy, do you think Mommy is proud of us?"

Ethan paused, a lump forming in his throat. "I'm sure she is, sweetheart. She's watching over us, and I believe she sees the strength and love that fills our hearts."

Lily smiled, her eyes reflecting a wisdom beyond her years. The journey of healing, marked by fragile steps forward, became a dance of progress and setbacks, each step imbued with the memory of Sarah and the promise of a future shaped by love and resilience.

In these moments, Ethan realized that the echoes of laughter, once distant and haunting, were evolving into a melody of hope. The whispers of dawn, now woven into the tapestry of their lives, guided them toward a tomorrow where healing, love, and the enduring spirit of family prevailed.

Chapter 5: A Community of Comfort

As Ethan and Lily continued their journey of healing, the sense of isolation that once enveloped them began to dissipate. A community of support emerged, a network of caring neighbors, friends, and fellow church members who extended comforting hands and open hearts.

One Sunday, as the church bells chimed, Ethan and Lily entered the familiar sanctuary. The echoes of their footsteps mingled with the hymns that filled the air. The pew, once a solemn reminder of absence, became a place of solace, surrounded by a community that embraced them with warmth.

The church community, recognizing the fragility of their journey, rallied around Ethan and Lily. Meals appeared on their doorstep, accompanied by handwritten notes of encouragement. Friends offered a listening ear, sharing their own stories of loss and resilience, creating a tapestry of shared experiences that provided comfort in the midst of sorrow.

In the evenings, the small group Bible study became a lifeline. The discussions, guided by the wisdom of faith, offered insights into navigating grief and finding strength in the promises of hope. The echoes of shared prayers resonated within the walls, creating a sacred space where sorrow was acknowledged but not defined them.

One particularly challenging day, as Lily struggled with the weight of missing her mother, a knock on the door revealed

Sarah's best friend, Rachel. With a knowing smile, Rachel held out a small gift – a photo album filled with cherished memories of Sarah. Each page turned was a glimpse into the laughter, joy, and love that defined their friendship.

"She loved you both so much," Rachel said, her voice filled with warmth. "And she would want you to remember the beautiful moments."

As Ethan and Lily flipped through the pages, laughter replaced tears, and the weight of silence lifted, if only for a moment. The community that surrounded them became a source of strength, a reminder that they were not alone in their journey.

In the weeks that followed, Ethan and Lily actively engaged with their newfound community. Together, they organized a memorial service to honor Sarah's memory, weaving together stories and anecdotes that celebrated her life. The church, adorned with flowers and flickering candles, echoed with a sense of closure and a shared commitment to embrace the future.

As they walked away from the service, hand in hand, Ethan and Lily felt a profound gratitude for the community that had become their extended family. The whispers of dawn, once gentle and distant, now echoed with the harmonies of shared sorrow and shared hope. In this community of comfort, they found the strength to face each new day, fortified by the bonds of friendship and the enduring promise that love transcends the boundaries of time and loss.

Chapter 6: Grasping at Memories

In the wake of the memorial service, Ethan and Lily found themselves navigating the delicate balance between holding onto cherished memories and embracing the prospect of a new chapter. The photo album from Rachel served as a tangible bridge between the past and the present, a collection of moments frozen in time, each image a testament to the love and laughter that defined their family.

The fragility of memories became evident as Ethan grappled with the challenge of preserving Sarah's essence for Lily. He spent evenings recounting stories, flipping through old photo albums, and revisiting familiar places that held sentimental value. The scent of lavender, once a bittersweet reminder, transformed into a comforting aroma that enveloped them as they relived shared moments.

One afternoon, as they sorted through Sarah's belongings, Lily discovered a box filled with handwritten letters. Intrigued, she opened one, revealing a letter Sarah had written for her on her fifth birthday. Tears welled up in Ethan's eyes as he listened to Sarah's words of love, encouragement, and dreams for Lily's future.

"Daddy, can we read more of Mommy's letters?" Lily asked, her eyes wide with curiosity.

Ethan nodded, realizing that these letters were a treasure trove of Sarah's thoughts and emotions. Together, they embarked on a journey through time, unraveling the words penned by a loving wife and mother. Each letter became a bridge connecting the past and the present, a testament to the enduring power of love that transcends the boundaries of life and death.

In the quiet moments of reflection, Ethan found solace in the written words that captured Sarah's essence. The letters became a source of guidance, a compass pointing toward a future where the echoes of her wisdom would continue to resonate. The weight of silence, once a heavy burden, transformed into a tapestry woven with the threads of love and shared memories.

As the days turned into weeks, Ethan and Lily began to infuse their home with the tangible reminders of Sarah's presence. Photographs adorned the walls, capturing moments of joy, laughter, and love. The fragrance of lavender became a comforting embrace, a reminder that love, in its purest form, endures beyond the physical realm.

One evening, as they sat on the porch, surrounded by the gentle hum of crickets and the soft glow of fireflies, Lily looked up at the stars. "Do you think Mommy is up there, Daddy?"

Ethan smiled, his heart full. "Yes, sweetheart. Mommy is like a star, shining down on us. Her love is a light that will always guide us, no matter where we are."

In the dance of memories and the whispers of dawn, Ethan and Lily found a delicate equilibrium. The past became a foundation upon which they built a future infused with the resilience of love. As they held onto the threads of memories, they stepped forward, hand in hand, into a tomorrow where the echoes of laughter and the whispers of dawn continued to shape their journey of healing.

Chapter 7: Whispers of Doubt

In the midst of their journey of healing, Ethan and Lily confronted moments of doubt that lingered like shadows, threatening to overshadow the progress they had made. The weight of grief, though gradually lifting, occasionally returned in waves, testing the resilience of their newfound strength.

One evening, as Ethan sat alone in the quiet of their living room, the echoes of laughter seemed distant. Doubt crept in, whispering insidious questions about the path ahead. Could he truly navigate this journey of single parenthood? Would Lily have the support and love she needed? Was he doing justice to Sarah's memory?

In the midst of these whispers of doubt, a familiar voice broke through the silence. Rachel, Sarah's best friend, appeared at the doorstep, a comforting presence in the face of uncertainty. Sensing Ethan's internal struggle, she spoke with empathy.

"Doubt is a part of the journey, Ethan. It's okay to question, to feel uncertain. Grief doesn't follow a linear path, and healing is a process, not a destination."

Her words resonated, offering a lifeline in the sea of uncertainty. Together, they revisited the letters Sarah had written, finding strength in the wisdom imparted through her words. Rachel became a pillar of support, helping Ethan navigate the complexities of single parenthood and assuring him that doubt, though present, didn't define the journey.

Lily, too, grappled with her own doubts. One day, she approached Ethan with a quizzical expression. "Daddy, do you think Mommy would be proud of me?"

Ethan knelt down, his eyes meeting Lily's. "Absolutely, sweetheart. Your strength, kindness, and laughter – those are all reflections of the love Mommy poured into your heart. She would be incredibly proud of the amazing person you're becoming."

As doubt gradually gave way to reassurance, Ethan realized that acknowledging uncertainty was not a sign of weakness but a testament to the complexity of grief. The whispers of dawn, once a distant promise, became a reminder that healing was a continuous journey, with moments of doubt serving as catalysts for growth.

In the weeks that followed, Ethan and Lily leaned on their support system, their community of comfort, to navigate the twists and turns of doubt. They embraced the uncertainty, recognizing that it was a natural part of the healing process. With each passing day, doubt transformed into determination, and the echoes of laughter, though at times hushed, became a resilient melody that underscored their journey.

As they faced the challenges of doubt together, Ethan and Lily discovered that within the uncertainties lay the potential for newfound strength and resilience. The whispers of dawn, now interwoven with the echoes of doubt, guided them forward, promising a future where love, faith, and the enduring power of family would illuminate the path ahead.

Chapter 8: The Language of Flowers

In the wake of doubt, Ethan and Lily discovered a profound language that transcended spoken words – the language of flowers. The garden, once a place of solace and shared moments with Sarah, transformed into a sanctuary where emotions found expression through the vibrant colors and delicate petals.

One afternoon, as they tended to the blossoms, Lily's fingers traced the velvety texture of a rose. "Mommy loved roses, didn't she, Daddy?"

Ethan nodded, a soft smile playing on his lips. "Yes, sweetheart. Roses held a special place in her heart. Each petal is like a whisper of love, a reminder of the beauty she brought into our lives."

As they explored the garden, they discovered the significance behind each flower. Daisies symbolized innocence and simplicity – qualities that defined Lily's spirit. Sunflowers stood tall, embodying strength and resilience. The language of flowers became a tangible connection to the past, a way to communicate with Sarah's memory in the gentle whispers of nature.

Ethan, inspired by the beauty that unfolded in their garden, decided to share this language with their community. He organized a flower planting event, inviting friends and neighbors to join in the creation of a community garden. Together, they planted tulips of hope, lilies of healing, and forget-me-nots to honor the memories of their loved ones.

As the community garden flourished, it became a living tapestry woven with the diverse stories of those who had experienced loss. The language of flowers became a universal conversation, a silent but powerful dialogue that conveyed the shared experiences of grief, healing, and the enduring bonds of love.

One evening, the community gathered in the garden for a candlelit ceremony. Each person held a flower, a symbol of their journey and the memories they carried. As the sun dipped below the horizon, casting a warm glow on the petals, Ethan spoke about the significance of their shared language.

"Each flower tells a story – a story of growth, resilience, and the beauty that emerges from the soil of loss. In this garden, we find solace in the language of flowers, a language that transcends words and connects us to the whispers of those we hold dear."

The ceremony concluded with a collective release of floating lanterns into the night sky. The flickering lights mirrored the resilience of their shared journey, illuminating the darkness with a message of hope.

In the language of flowers, Ethan and Lily discovered a powerful means of expression, a way to communicate their emotions and honor the memory of Sarah. As they walked away from the garden, hand in hand, the whispers of dawn echoed through the petals, promising a future where love and the language of flowers continued to bloom, even in the face of loss.

Chapter 9: A Hand to Hold

With the language of flowers having woven its way into the fabric of their lives, Ethan and Lily continued their journey of healing, finding strength in the delicate petals that whispered messages of hope and resilience. However, as they navigated the complexities of grief, they realized that the power of healing extended beyond the garden; it was also found in the simple act of offering and receiving a hand to hold.

One day, as Ethan and Lily walked through the neighborhood, they noticed a new family moving in next door. The air was filled with the sounds of laughter and the clatter of boxes being unpacked. A sense of anticipation lingered, and Ethan couldn't help but feel a mixture of nostalgia and curiosity about the new neighbors.

A few days later, as Ethan tended to the garden, he noticed the neighbor's daughter, Emily, standing by the fence, gazing at the flowers. Lily, ever friendly, approached her with a warm smile.

"Hi, I'm Lily. Do you want to see our garden?" she asked.

Emily nodded, and soon the three of them were exploring the vibrant blooms. In the language of flowers, they found a common ground, a bridge that connected their worlds. The garden, once a source of solace for Ethan and Lily, became a place of shared laughter and budding friendship.

As the days passed, Ethan and Lily extended a hand of welcome to the new neighbors. Emily's parents, Lisa and Michael, shared stories of their own journey, having recently relocated to the neighborhood. The camaraderie that emerged echoed the sentiment that, in the ebb and flow of life, the strength of community lay in the willingness to offer a hand to hold.

One evening, as the sun dipped below the horizon, Ethan, Lily, and their new friends gathered in the garden for a simple dinner. The fragrance of blooming flowers mingled with the aroma of homemade dishes, creating an atmosphere of warmth and connection. Amidst the laughter and shared stories, Ethan realized the profound impact of extending a hand to hold – a gesture that went beyond words, expressing empathy, support, and a shared understanding of the journey each had undertaken. The newfound friendship became a testament to the resilience of the human spirit. In their shared experiences of grief and healing, Ethan, Lily, and their neighbors discovered the strength that emerges when hands are joined in solidarity. The whispers of dawn, once distant and ethereal, now reverberated through the laughter and shared moments, promising a future where the bonds of friendship and the enduring power of connection would continue to blossom, much like the flowers in their garden.

Chapter 10: Unexpected Laughter

As the days unfolded, the bond between Ethan, Lily, and their newfound neighbors, Lisa, Michael, and Emily, deepened. The garden that once stood as a symbol of solace transformed into a vibrant testament to the resilience of shared laughter and unexpected joy.

One weekend, the families decided to organize a neighborhood barbecue. The air was filled with the sizzle of the grill, children's laughter, and the hum of lively conversations. The fragrant scent of flowers in full bloom mingled with the aroma of grilled delicacies, creating an atmosphere of warmth and camaraderie.

As the evening unfolded, Ethan couldn't help but marvel at the transformation their lives had undergone. The weight of grief, though not forgotten, had given way to shared moments of joy and unexpected laughter. The language of flowers, once a silent solace, now resonated with the vivacious energy of a community coming together.

Amidst the shared meals and laughter, Ethan and Lily discovered a new facet of healing – the healing that arises when unexpected joy becomes a part of the tapestry of life. Emily and Lily, their friendship blossoming, played together, their laughter echoing through the neighborhood like a melody of happiness.

In the midst of the barbecue, Lisa shared a heartfelt sentiment with Ethan. "Your family has brought so much warmth and joy to our lives. We feel blessed to be a part of this community."

Ethan smiled, grateful for the unexpected connections that had emerged from the garden of healing. The whispers of dawn, once soft and distant, now resonated with the harmonies of shared laughter and the promise of a future where joy and resilience intertwined.

As the evening drew to a close, the families gathered around a fire pit, the flickering flames casting a warm glow on their faces. Ethan, holding Lily close, realized that healing wasn't just about navigating grief; it was also about allowing space for unexpected moments of joy to bloom.

This chapter closes with the image of neighbors, once strangers, now bound by shared laughter and a newfound sense of community. The language of flowers, infused with the vibrant hues of friendship, continued to tell a story of resilience, hope, and the enduring power of unexpected joy.

Chapter 11: Footprints in the Sand

The warmth of summer transitioned into the gentle embrace of autumn, and as the leaves began to paint the neighborhood in hues of gold and red, Ethan and Lily found themselves reflecting on the footprints they had left on the sands of time. The whispers of dawn, which once beckoned them towards healing, now carried echoes of gratitude for the unexpected laughter and the bonds of friendship that had bloomed.

One crisp autumn afternoon, as Ethan and Lily strolled through the neighborhood, the fallen leaves crunched beneath their feet, leaving a trail of memories in their wake. The footprints in the sand of time mirrored the journey of healing, each step an imprint of resilience and growth.

Ethan's gaze wandered to the garden, now adorned with autumn blooms. The language of flowers, once vibrant in the summer, took on new shades of meaning. Chrysanthemums symbolized resilience, while marigolds represented the beauty found in overcoming challenges. The garden, a living testament to their journey, now stood as a visual poem of gratitude for the footprints they had imprinted upon its soil.

As they approached their home, Ethan noticed a small plaque on the porch, a gift from their neighbors. It read, "In gratitude for laughter shared and footprints left in the sands of time. Love, Lisa, Michael, and Emily."

Touched by the sentiment, Ethan felt a profound appreciation for the unexpected connections that had blossomed in the wake of loss. The footprints they had left, both literal and metaphorical, were a testament to the resilience of the human spirit and the enduring power of community.

That evening, as they gathered in the garden with their neighbors, a sense of gratitude permeated the air. The flickering candles and the gentle rustle of leaves created an ambiance of reflection and shared appreciation. Each person present, their lives interwoven like the threads of a tapestry, acknowledged the footprints they had left on each other's hearts.

In the quiet moments of gratitude, Ethan and Lily realized that healing wasn't just an individual journey; it was a collective experience, shaped by the footprints of those who walked alongside them. The whispers of dawn, though softer now, carried the promise that footprints, like memories, endure, creating a legacy of love and resilience that transcends the sands of time.

As the chapter drew to a close, Ethan and Lily embraced the beauty of the present moment, grateful for the footprints they had left and those that had guided them along the path of healing. The whispers of dawn, a gentle lullaby, promised that the journey, though marked by loss, was also illuminated by the enduring light of love and shared memories.

Chapter 12: Questions in the Starlight

As the year drew to a close, Ethan and Lily found themselves beneath the expansive canvas of a starlit sky, contemplating the mysteries that unfolded in the tapestry of their lives. The garden, once a sanctuary of solace, now became a space for quiet reflection, illuminated by the soft glow of twinkling stars.

One evening, as Ethan and Lily sat on the porch, wrapped in blankets against the crisp night air, Lily gazed up at the sky. "Daddy, do you think Mommy can see the stars from where she is?"

Ethan smiled, his eyes reflecting the starlight. "I'm sure she can, sweetheart. The stars are like windows to the heavens, and I like to believe that Mommy watches over us from one of them."

Lily nodded, her gaze fixed on a particularly bright star. "What do you think she'd say if we could talk to her, Daddy?"

Ethan pondered for a moment before responding, "I think she'd tell us that she's proud of us, that she loves us more than words can express. And maybe, just maybe, she'd share a bit of the starlight with us to guide our way."

The quiet conversation under the starlit sky opened a space for contemplation, and Ethan found himself asking questions of his own. Questions about the meaning of life, the interconnectedness of memories, and the enduring impact of love.

In the weeks that followed, Ethan and Lily delved into books about astronomy and the wonders of the universe. The language of stars became a new fascination, a way to connect with the vastness of existence and the beauty of the unknown. The garden, now adorned with small star-shaped lanterns, became a celestial haven, a reminder that even in the face of loss, there was a cosmic beauty that transcended the boundaries of earthly sorrow.

One night, as they stargazed in the garden, Ethan whispered his thoughts into the night air, a silent conversation with the universe. Lily, ever curious, asked, "Daddy, do you think we'll ever get answers to all our questions?"

Ethan chuckled softly, ruffling Lily's hair. "Some questions may not have clear answers, sweetheart. But the beauty is in the journey of asking, exploring, and finding meaning in the mysteries that unfold around us."

In the quiet moments of starlight contemplation, Ethan and Lily discovered that questions, much like stars in the night sky, were guideposts on their journey of continuous learning. The whispers of dawn, though now hushed, carried the promise that the pursuit of understanding, fueled by love and curiosity, would illuminate their path, just as the stars illuminated the vastness of the cosmic canvas above.

Chapter 13: Glimmers of Forgiveness

As the pages of time turned, Ethan and Lily found themselves standing at the threshold of a new year, a time for reflection and renewal. In the quiet moments of transition, they realized that forgiveness was a crucial step in their journey of healing. The garden, now adorned with winter blooms, became a symbolic landscape for the blooming glimmers of forgiveness.

One frost-kissed morning, as they strolled through the garden, Lily noticed a wilted flower. "Daddy, can we bring it back to life?" Ethan smiled at her determination. Together, they carefully nurtured the fragile bloom, providing warmth and tender care. In the process, they discovered the parallels between reviving a wilted flower and fostering forgiveness—a delicate, intentional act that required patience, understanding, and the warmth of love.

Forgiveness, Ethan realized, was not only about releasing the pain of the past but also about cultivating a space for new growth. The wilted flower, now rejuvenated, stood as a living testament to the transformative power of compassion and understanding.

In the spirit of forgiveness, Ethan decided to visit Sarah's resting place. The winter landscape, blanketed in snow, created a serene backdrop for reflection. As he stood there, surrounded by a quiet stillness, Ethan found the strength to let go of lingering resentment and embrace the beauty of forgiveness.

Back in the garden, Lily held a small ceremony, placing a forgiven flower in the ground as a symbol of their journey toward healing. The whispers of dawn, though softer now, carried the promise that forgiveness was not only an act of grace towards others but also a gift they gave themselves—a gift that allowed them to move forward with lighter hearts.

In the weeks that followed, Ethan and Lily consciously embraced the practice of forgiveness in their daily lives. The garden, once a sanctuary for solitary reflection, now became a communal space where the seeds of forgiveness were sown, and the blooms of understanding began to unfurl.

One evening, as they sat by the fireplace, Lily looked at Ethan with a thoughtful expression. "Daddy, do you think forgiveness is a one-time thing, or do we have to forgive over and over?"

Ethan considered her question before responding, "Forgiveness is a journey, sweetheart. Sometimes, we may need to forgive again and again as we navigate life's twists and turns. It's a continuous practice that leads to inner peace and growth."

In the glimmers of forgiveness, Ethan and Lily found a renewed sense of freedom. The echoes of laughter, the whispers of dawn, and the language of flowers all converged in the garden, creating a tapestry woven with threads of healing, understanding, and the transformative beauty of forgiveness.

Chapter 14: A Shared Symphony

As winter embraced the world in a tranquil hush, Ethan and Lily discovered the profound beauty that emerged when their individual journeys harmonized into a shared symphony. The garden, adorned with delicate frost and resilient winter blooms, became a testament to the intricate melodies woven from the threads of their healing.

One snowy afternoon, Ethan and Lily decided to create a winter symphony in the garden. Armed with small chimes, they hung them among the branches of dormant trees, allowing the wind to compose its own ethereal melody. The chimes danced and sang, creating a symphony of delicate notes that echoed through the serene landscape.

In the shared symphony of nature, Ethan and Lily found a metaphor for their interconnected lives. Each note, like an individual journey, contributed to the harmonious tapestry of their shared experience. The garden, now adorned with winter chimes, became a sanctuary where the echoes of individual healing resonated in unison.

Inspired by their winter symphony, Ethan decided to organize a community gathering in the garden. Neighbors, friends, and their newfound companions, Lisa, Michael, and Emily, joined in the celebration of shared healing and resilience. The air filled with laughter, stories, and the gentle tinkling of chimes, creating an atmosphere of unity and connection.

As they stood together in the garden, surrounded by the winter beauty, Ethan addressed the gathering. "In the symphony of life, each of us plays a unique part. Our individual journeys, marked by loss and healing, come together to create a shared melody—a symphony of love, friendship, and the enduring power of community."

The shared symphony became a poignant reminder that healing wasn't a solitary endeavor but a collaborative dance with the rhythms of life. The whispers of dawn, though softer now, carried the promise that in unity, they would find strength and resilience to face the unfolding chapters of their lives.

In the weeks that followed, Ethan, Lily, and their community continued to nurture the garden, not just as a place of solace but as a living testament to the shared symphony of healing. The winter chimes, now a permanent fixture, became a symbol of the interconnected threads that bound them together, creating a melody that transcended the boundaries of grief and loss.

As the chapter concluded, Ethan and Lily stood in the garden, listening to the harmonious notes of their winter symphony. The echoes of laughter, the language of flowers, the whispers of dawn—all converged in this shared melody, promising a future where the threads of their lives would continue to weave a tapestry of resilience, love, and the enduring beauty of togetherness.

Chapter 15: Unveiling Secrets

As the tapestry of their lives unfolded, Ethan and Lily found themselves standing at the crossroads of discovery. The garden, now adorned with the promise of spring, became a place of revelation—a sanctuary where secrets, long held within the recesses of their hearts, were unveiled.

One day, as they tended to the blossoming flowers, Lily looked at Ethan with a curious glint in her eyes. "Daddy, do you think Mommy left us any secrets to discover?"

Ethan pondered the question before responding, "I believe your mom left us a treasure trove of memories and, perhaps, some surprises along the way. Let's explore and see what secrets the garden holds."

Inspired by Lily's curiosity, they embarked on a journey of discovery within the garden. Among the vibrant blooms, they uncovered small notes tucked beneath leaves and nestled within the petals. Each note held a message—a piece of Sarah's heart revealed through written words.

In one note, she expressed her dreams for Lily's future. In another, she shared a favorite recipe, a secret ingredient being her love. The garden, it seemed, was a living testament to the secrets Sarah had planted, waiting to be discovered in moments of reflection and shared exploration.

The unveiling of secrets extended beyond the garden. In Sarah's study, Ethan stumbled upon a journal filled with her thoughts, dreams, and reflections on their life together. As he turned the pages, he discovered a side of Sarah he hadn't fully known—a woman of depth, resilience, and unwavering love.

In the midst of these revelations, Ethan realized that the secrets they unveiled weren't just about Sarah; they were also about the evolving journey of healing and self-discovery. The garden, once a place of solace, became a symbol of the ongoing narrative, where each bloom held the potential for a new secret to be unraveled.

One evening, as they sat in the garden, surrounded by the fragrance of blossoms, Lily spoke softly, "I think Mommy left us these secrets so we could keep discovering her love, over and over again."

Ethan nodded, touched by Lily's insight. The whispers of dawn, though gentler now, carried the promise that the unveiling of secrets was an ongoing process—a continuous journey of connection and understanding.

In the weeks that followed, Ethan and Lily continued to explore the garden and Sarah's notes, finding joy in the unfolding secrets left behind. The echoes of laughter, the language of flowers, the shared symphony, and now the unveiling of secrets—all converged in the garden, creating a rich tapestry that told the story of love, loss, and the enduring legacy of a life well-lived.

Chapter 16: The Crossroads of Choice

As the seasons cycled through the garden, Ethan and Lily found themselves at a significant crossroads—a juncture where choices would shape the trajectory of their lives. The garden, adorned with the vibrant hues of summer, became a reflective space where the paths of the past converged with the possibilities of the future.

One afternoon, as they sat in the shade of a blooming tree, Lily looked up at Ethan with a contemplative gaze. "Daddy, what do you think Mommy would want us to do with the garden? Should we keep it the same, or make changes?"

Ethan considered the question, recognizing the significance of the choice ahead. "Your mom loved this garden because it was a place of beauty, growth, and shared memories. I believe she would want us to honor those values, whether we keep it the same or make changes that reflect our own journey."

Inspired by their conversation, Ethan and Lily decided to explore new additions to the garden—a symbolic representation of the choices they were making in their lives. They planted a flowering tree in memory of Sarah, symbolizing the enduring strength of their roots. They also added a bench, a place for quiet reflection and shared moments.

The garden, once a static landscape, now reflected the evolving narrative of their healing journey. The crossroads of choice became a transformative space where the threads of the past interwove with the possibilities of the present.

In the process of making choices for the garden, Ethan also found himself at a professional crossroads. Reflecting on his career as an IT professional, he contemplated the possibility of taking on new challenges, pursuing further education, or even exploring entrepreneurial endeavors. The whispers of dawn, though quieter now, carried the promise that continuous learning and growth were inherent to the journey.

Lily, too, faced choices in her young life—decisions about school, hobbies, and the kind of person she aspired to become. As father and daughter navigated their respective crossroads, they found solace in the shared understanding that choices, though daunting, were the building blocks of a dynamic and fulfilling life.

One evening, as they stood in the garden, surrounded by the fruits of their choices, Ethan addressed Lily, "Life is a series of crossroads, sweetheart. Each choice we make shapes our journey, but what's important is the intention and love we put into those choices."

As the chapter concluded, Ethan and Lily embraced the transformative power of their choices. The echoes of laughter, the language of flowers, the shared symphony, the unveiling of secrets, and now the crossroads of choice—all converged in the garden, creating a mosaic of resilience, growth, and the enduring beauty of intentional living.

Chapter 17: Faith Under Fire

Amidst the vibrant blooms of summer, Ethan and Lily found themselves facing challenges that tested the core of their faith. The garden, once a haven of solace, now became a crucible where the flames of adversity forged the strength to endure.

One evening, as they gathered in the garden, a sudden storm rolled in, with winds whipping through the blossoms and rain pelting down like tears from the heavens. Ethan, shielding Lily from the elements, felt a surge of helplessness, mirroring the tumultuous emotions within.

In the aftermath of the storm, they surveyed the garden—flowers battered but resilient, soil drenched but nourished. In the face of adversity, the garden stood as a metaphor for their own journey—weathered but undefeated, ready to bloom again.

The challenges extended beyond the physical realm. Lily, in her young life, faced situations that tested her understanding of the world. Ethan, in turn, grappled with the complexities of parenthood and the responsibility of nurturing faith in the midst of uncertainty.

In their shared moments of reflection, Ethan and Lily turned to the faith that had sustained them through loss. They sought solace in prayer, drawing strength from the unwavering belief that even in the midst of storms, there existed a promise of renewal and growth.

As they tended to the garden, Ethan spoke to Lily about the concept of faith under fire. "Our faith, much like the garden, faces challenges. It's in those moments of trial that the true essence of our beliefs is tested. But remember, just as the garden blooms again after a storm, so does our faith have the resilience to endure."

In the weeks that followed, they continued to nurture the garden, witnessing the gradual resurgence of life. The echoes of laughter, the language of flowers, the shared symphony, the unveiling of secrets, the crossroads of choice—all now converged in the garden, serving as a testament to the enduring nature of faith.

One quiet evening, as the sun dipped below the horizon, Ethan and Lily stood in the garden, a place where faith had been tested and reaffirmed. The whispers of dawn, though softer now, carried the assurance that faith, tempered by the fires of adversity, could withstand the storms of life, promising a future where the garden of their hearts would continue to bloom with the flowers of resilience and enduring belief.

Chapter 18: Broken Pieces Mending

In the dappled glow of autumn, Ethan and Lily found themselves intricately weaving the broken pieces of their hearts into a mosaic of healing. The garden, once a canvas of vibrant blooms, now reflected the delicate process of mending—a testimony to the resilience that emerged from the fractures of loss and challenges.

As they strolled through the garden, fallen leaves crunching beneath their feet, Ethan noticed a broken planter. The shards of pottery lay scattered, mirroring the fragments of their own lives. Instead of discarding the broken pieces, they decided to mend the planter together.

Seated on the porch, they carefully arranged the shattered fragments, gluing them back together with a purposeful gentleness. In the act of restoration, Ethan and Lily discovered the beauty that emerged when broken pieces were treated with care and reverence.

The broken planter, once a symbol of fragility, now stood as a transformed piece of art—a mosaic that bore the marks of healing. The garden, with its mended planter and the changing hues of autumn, became a sanctuary where broken pieces were not discarded but rather embraced as integral parts of their evolving narrative.

In the process of mending physical and metaphorical fragments, Ethan found himself reflecting on the interconnectedness of healing and growth. The echoes of laughter, the language of flowers, the shared symphony, the unveiling of secrets, the crossroads of choice, and the faith under fire—all converged in the garden, telling a story of resilience woven from the threads of brokenness.

Lily, too, grasped the concept of broken pieces mending as they navigated the challenges of life together. In her innocence, she spoke words that resonated deeply with Ethan, "Daddy, it's like the garden and us. We're putting the broken pieces back together, and it makes something beautiful."

As autumn unfolded, Ethan and Lily continued to mend not only the garden but also the intangible fragments of their hearts. The whispers of dawn, though quieter now, carried the promise that from brokenness emerged a mosaic of strength and beauty—a testament to the enduring power of love and healing.

Chapter 19: Dancing in the Rain

As winter relinquished its hold, Ethan and Lily found themselves embracing the onset of spring with a newfound sense of joy and resilience. The garden, adorned with the first blooms of the season, became a canvas for the dance of life—a celebration that echoed the rhythm of healing and renewal.

One rainy afternoon, as the garden embraced the gentle showers, Ethan and Lily decided to step outside. They stood amidst the raindrops, their faces turned upwards, feeling the cool embrace of water on their skin. The garden, drenched in rain, came alive with vibrant colors and fragrances, a testament to the beauty that emerged even in the midst of storms. In the dance of raindrops, Ethan and Lily found a metaphor for their own journey. Each raindrop, a symbol of life's challenges, held the potential to nourish and revitalize. They twirled and laughed in the garden, a dance that mirrored the resilience born from the storms they had weathered.

Inspired by their spontaneous dance, they decided to plant a variety of flowers that flourished in the rain. The garden, now a tapestry of colors and fragrances, became a living testament to the idea that even in adversity, there existed the potential for growth and beauty.

In the weeks that followed, Ethan and Lily continued to dance in the rain, both literally and metaphorically. The echoes of laughter, the language of flowers, the shared symphony, the unveiling of secrets, the crossroads of choice, the faith under fire, the broken pieces mending—all converged in the garden, creating a kaleidoscope of experiences that told a story of resilience, joy, and the enduring spirit of life.

One evening, as the sun set, casting a warm glow over the rain-kissed garden, Ethan looked at Lily with a profound sense of gratitude. "Life, much like this dance in the rain, is about finding joy in the midst of challenges. It's about embracing the moments of beauty that arise, even when the storms are fierce."

As the chapter drew to a close, Ethan and Lily stood in the garden, rain-kissed and resilient. The whispers of dawn, though softer now, carried the promise that in the dance of life, there existed a profound beauty that transcended the storms, reminding them that even in the rain, there was a melody of joy waiting to be embraced.

Chapter 20: The Art of Letting Go

With the advent of summer, Ethan and Lily found themselves immersed in the art of letting go—a transformative process that allowed them to release the weight of the past and embrace the unfolding possibilities of the present. The garden, now in full bloom, became a metaphorical canvas where the strokes of letting go painted a portrait of freedom and renewal.

One day, as they tended to the garden, Lily noticed a cluster of blossoms that had outgrown their original space. She turned to Ethan with a thoughtful expression, "Daddy, do you think it's time to let some flowers go, so they can find new places to bloom?"

Ethan nodded, recognizing the depth of Lily's insight. Together, they carefully selected a few vibrant blossoms and replanted them in different areas of the garden. In the act of letting go, they witnessed the flowers flourish in their newfound spaces, a visual representation of the beauty that emerged when one embraced change.

Inspired by this lesson from the garden, Ethan began to declutter their home, parting with items that held memories but no longer served a purpose. The process of letting go extended beyond the physical realm, as he found himself releasing lingering attachments to grief and embracing the freedom that came with acceptance.

In the midst of letting go, Lily also faced her own challenges of transitioning to a new phase in her school life. As a father, Ethan encouraged her to release any anxieties and trust in her ability to adapt. The whispers of dawn, though softer now, carried the promise that letting go was not a loss but a liberation—a stepping stone towards new beginnings.

As they sat in the garden, surrounded by the colors of summer, Ethan spoke to Lily about the art of letting go. "Life is a series of cycles, sweetheart. Just as flowers need space to bloom, we, too, need to release what no longer serves us to make room for new growth."

In the weeks that followed, Ethan and Lily continued to practice the art of letting go, both in the garden and in their lives. The echoes of laughter, the language of flowers, the shared symphony, the unveiling of secrets, the crossroads of choice, the faith under fire, the broken pieces mending, the dancing in the rain—all converged in the garden, creating a tapestry woven with the threads of liberation, acceptance, and the enduring beauty of renewal.

As the chapter drew to a close, Ethan and Lily stood in the garden, a place where the art of letting go had become a transformative dance with the ever-changing rhythms of life. The whispers of dawn, though gentler now, carried the assurance that in releasing the past, they were creating space for a future where the garden of their hearts could continue to bloom with the colors of hope and resilience.

Chapter 21: A Mother's Love Endures

Amidst the golden hues of late summer, Ethan and Lily found themselves exploring the profound depth of a mother's love—an enduring force that transcended the boundaries of time and loss. The garden, with its blossoming flowers and whispering leaves, became a sacred space where the echoes of Sarah's love reverberated, offering solace and guidance.

One evening, as the sun dipped below the horizon, casting a warm glow over the garden, Lily spoke softly, "Daddy, do you think Mommy still loves us from wherever she is?" Ethan knelt beside Lily, his eyes reflecting the hues of sunset. "Absolutely, sweetheart. A mother's love is timeless. Even though Mommy is no longer with us, her love continues to surround and guide us. It's in the gentle breeze, the blooming flowers, and every beautiful moment we share."

Inspired by Lily's question, they decided to create a memorial space in the garden—a place where they could honor and celebrate Sarah's enduring love. They planted her favorite flowers, adorned the area with cherished mementos, and created a small bench for moments of quiet reflection.

In this sacred corner of the garden, Ethan and Lily often sat, sharing stories about Sarah, reminiscing about the laughter they once shared as a family. The whispers of dawn, though softer now, carried the promise that love, in its purest form, was a timeless bond that transcended physical presence.

As they tended to the memorial garden, Lily discovered a collection of letters that Sarah had written for her and Ethan. Each letter, penned with love and wisdom, served as a poignant reminder of a mother's enduring presence in their lives. The letters became treasures, providing comfort and guidance in moments of uncertainty.

In the weeks that followed, Ethan and Lily found solace in the memorial garden, a space where Sarah's love felt palpable. The echoes of laughter, the language of flowers, the shared symphony, the unveiling of secrets, the crossroads of choice, the faith under fire, the broken pieces mending, the dancing in the rain, the art of letting go—all converged in this sacred space, creating a tapestry woven with threads of love and remembrance.

One night, as fireflies danced around the garden, Ethan whispered to Lily, "A mother's love endures, my dear. It's a guiding light that continues to shine in our hearts, connecting us with the beautiful memories we shared and the infinite love that transcends the boundaries of time and space."

As the chapter concluded, Ethan and Lily sat in the memorial garden, surrounded by the gentle embrace of Sarah's enduring love. The whispers of dawn, though quieter now, carried the assurance that love, like a timeless melody, would continue to weave its harmonious chords through the garden of their lives.

Chapter 22: Facing the Unknown

In the crisp air of early autumn, Ethan and Lily found themselves standing at the threshold of the unknown—an inevitable frontier that beckoned with both trepidation and the promise of new discoveries. The garden, with its leaves transforming into shades of amber and gold, became a symbol of the evolving seasons of life, where facing the unknown was an essential part of the journey.

One afternoon, as they raked fallen leaves and tended to the garden's autumnal transformation, Lily looked up at Ethan with a curious expression. "Daddy, what do you think is waiting for us in the unknown future?"

Ethan paused, appreciating the depth of Lily's question. "The unknown is like a vast garden, sweetheart. It holds the seeds of endless possibilities, challenges, and beautiful moments yet to bloom. We may not know exactly what awaits us, but with faith, resilience, and an open heart, we can navigate this uncharted territory."

Inspired by their conversation, they decided to plant bulbs in the garden—a symbolic act of faith in the future. As they gently buried the bulbs beneath the soil, Ethan spoke about the parallels between gardening and facing the unknown. "Just as these bulbs will bloom into beautiful flowers in the spring, our journey into the unknown holds the potential for growth, renewal, and unexpected beauty."

In the weeks that followed, Ethan and Lily faced various uncertainties, both personally and professionally. Lily navigated the challenges of school, while Ethan considered new opportunities in his career. The echoes of laughter, the language of flowers, the shared symphony, the unveiling of secrets, the crossroads of choice, the faith under fire, the broken pieces mending, the dancing in the rain, the art of letting go, the enduring love of a mother—all converged in the garden, becoming a source of strength as they embraced the unknown.

One evening, as they sat by a crackling fire pit in the garden, Ethan shared his thoughts with Lily. "Facing the unknown can be daunting, but it's also where we find the potential for growth and transformation. Just like the changing seasons in the garden, our lives are filled with cycles of change, and it's up to us to adapt and flourish."

As the flames flickered and the night settled around them, Ethan and Lily embraced the uncertainties of the future, finding solace in the knowledge that the garden of their lives, with its ever-changing landscape, held the promise of new beginnings and uncharted beauty. The whispers of dawn, though softer now, carried the assurance that in facing the unknown, they were embarking on a journey filled with the potential for growth, resilience, and the blossoming of unforeseen joys.

Chapter 23: A Leap of Faith

As autumn embraced the garden in a tapestry of warm hues, Ethan and Lily found themselves standing at the precipice of a significant decision—a moment that required a leap of faith into the unknown. The garden, with its leaves rustling in the crisp breeze, became a reflective space where the courage to take risks and trust in the journey ahead was paramount.

One evening, as they sat on the porch, sipping warm tea and watching the leaves dance in the wind, Lily turned to Ethan with a determined expression. "Daddy, what if we try something new? Something that challenges us and takes us out of our comfort zone."

Ethan contemplated Lily's words, realizing the profound truth in her suggestion. "Sweetheart, sometimes the most beautiful flowers bloom when the seeds are planted in unfamiliar soil. What do you have in mind?"

Encouraged by her father's openness, Lily shared her dream of starting a small community garden project—a space where neighbors and friends could come together, share experiences, and cultivate a sense of unity. The idea resonated deeply with Ethan, and together, they decided to take a leap of faith into this new endeavor.

In the weeks that followed, Ethan and Lily worked tirelessly to bring their community garden vision to life. The echoes of laughter, the language of flowers, the shared symphony, the unveiling of secrets, the crossroads of choice, the faith under fire, the broken pieces mending, the dancing in the rain, the art of letting go, the enduring love of a mother, facing the unknown—a mosaic of experiences converged in the garden, providing the foundation for their shared leap of faith.

The community embraced the project, and the garden soon became a vibrant hub of shared stories, laughter, and a sense of belonging. In the heart of the unknown, Ethan and Lily discovered the transformative power of taking risks, cultivating connections, and fostering growth in the most unexpected places.

One evening, as they walked through the flourishing community garden, Ethan looked at Lily with pride. "You had a vision, and together, we took a leap of faith. Look at the beauty we've created—a space where people come together, nurture the soil, and watch as their efforts blossom into something extraordinary."

As the chapter drew to a close, Ethan and Lily stood in the midst of the community garden, a testament to the potential that unfolds when one embraces the unknown with an open heart. The whispers of dawn, though softer now, carried the promise that in taking leaps of faith, they were not only enriching their own lives but also sowing seeds of inspiration and unity in the lives of those around them.

Chapter 24: The Promise of Dawn

In the gentle embrace of late autumn, Ethan and Lily found themselves reflecting on the journey that had brought them to this transformative moment. The garden, adorned with the last remnants of fall foliage, became a canvas upon which the lessons of resilience, growth, and the enduring power of love were painted.

As they walked through the garden, Lily spoke with a quiet certainty, "Daddy, I've learned so much from the garden. It's like a teacher, guiding us through the seasons of life."

Ethan smiled, appreciating the wisdom in Lily's words. "Indeed, sweetheart. The garden has been our companion, teaching us about the beauty of change, the importance of nurturing growth, and the promise of new beginnings. What lessons do you carry in your heart?"

Lily paused, her gaze wandering over the garden. "I've learned that even in the coldest winters, the promise of spring is always there. No matter how tough the storms, the garden keeps blooming. It's like the whispers of dawn, Daddy—the assurance that after every dark night, there's a new day waiting to dawn."

Inspired by Lily's insight, they decided to plant winter-blooming flowers, a symbolic gesture of their journey's cyclical nature. The echoes of laughter, the language of flowers, the shared symphony, the unveiling of secrets, the crossroads of choice, the faith under fire, the broken pieces mending, the dancing in the rain, the art of letting go, the enduring love of a mother, facing the unknown, a leap of faith—a culmination of experiences converged in the garden, creating a mosaic that told the story of their shared growth.

As winter settled in, Ethan and Lily continued to find warmth and inspiration in the quiet beauty of the garden. The whispers of dawn, though softer now, carried the assurance that the promise of a new day remained constant—an ever-present beacon of hope and renewal.

On a crisp morning, as they stood in the garden, a subtle light began to break on the horizon. Ethan looked at Lily with a tender smile. "The promise of dawn, my dear. It's a reminder that with each passing season, we have the opportunity to embrace new beginnings, to bloom and flourish, just like the garden."

As the chapter drew to a close, Ethan and Lily stood in the winter-kissed garden, surrounded by the echoes of their journey. The whispers of dawn, though quieter now, carried the promise that the garden of their lives would continue to bloom with the flowers of resilience, hope, and the enduring beauty of a love that transcended the changing seasons.

Chapter 25: Love's Second Chorus

As winter began to loosen its grip, Ethan and Lily found themselves standing on the cusp of a new chapter—one where the echoes of their journey resonated with the vibrant melodies of love's enduring chorus. The garden, awakening from its winter slumber, became a stage upon which the symphony of their shared experiences played, each note a testament to the strength of their bond.

One sunny afternoon, as they worked together to prepare the garden for the approaching spring, Lily spoke with a thoughtful expression, "Daddy, do you think love can have a second chorus? Like a song that keeps playing, evolving with each verse."

Ethan considered Lily's metaphor, realizing the depth of her insight. "Absolutely, sweetheart. Love, much like a timeless melody, has the power to weave new verses into our lives. As we grow, face challenges, and embrace new beginnings, the chorus of love continues, harmonizing with the ever-changing rhythms of our journey."

Inspired by their conversation, they decided to plant perennial flowers—a symbol of love that endured through the changing seasons. The garden, with its awakening blooms, became a living canvas where the echoes of laughter, the language of flowers, the shared symphony, the unveiling of secrets, the crossroads of choice, the faith under fire, the broken pieces mending, the dancing in the rain, the art of letting go, the enduring love of a mother, facing the unknown, a leap of faith, the promise of dawn—all converged in a crescendo of love's second chorus.

In the weeks that followed, Ethan and Lily embraced the evolving nature of their relationship. Love, once rooted in the laughter of shared moments, now blossomed into a deeper understanding—one that weathered storms and celebrated the blossoming of new joys.

As they sat in the garden, basking in the warmth of the sun, Ethan spoke to Lily about love's second chorus. "Every chapter of life brings new melodies, and love is the harmonizing force that connects them all. It's a beautiful, evolving song that we create together."

With the garden as their witness, Ethan and Lily continued to nurture the symphony of their relationship. The whispers of dawn, though softer now, carried the assurance that love's second chorus, like a timeless melody, would continue to play, weaving its harmonious chords through the garden of their shared journey.

Chapter 26: Whispers of Forever

In the embrace of the first buds of spring, Ethan and Lily found themselves standing at the culmination of their transformative journey—a moment where the garden and their lives intertwined, echoing with the timeless whispers of forever. The air was filled with the promise of renewal, and the garden, adorned with blossoming flowers, became a living tapestry that mirrored the beauty of their shared experiences.

As they wandered through the garden, Lily spoke with a sense of contentment, "Daddy, it feels like the garden has grown with us. Every flower, every season, tells a story—a story of resilience, love, and the whispers of forever."

Ethan nodded, recognizing the profound truth in Lily's words. "Sweetheart, the garden is a reflection of our journey. Each petal, each leaf, is a page in the story of our lives. And just as the garden continues to bloom, our story unfolds with new chapters, guided by the whispers of forever."

Inspired by their conversation, they decided to create a memorial stone at the heart of the garden—a place where the echoes of their journey could be forever engraved. They inscribed it with words that captured the essence of their experiences, a testament to the enduring beauty of their shared story.

In the weeks that followed, Ethan and Lily continued to nurture the garden, finding solace and joy in its ever-changing beauty. The echoes of laughter, the language of flowers, the shared symphony, the unveiling of secrets, the crossroads of choice, the faith under fire, the broken pieces mending, the dancing in the rain, the art of letting go, the enduring love of a mother, facing the unknown, a leap of faith, the promise of dawn, love's second chorus—all converged in the garden, creating a legacy that whispered of forever.

One evening, as the sun dipped below the horizon, casting a warm glow over the garden, Ethan looked at Lily with a profound sense of gratitude. "Our journey, Lily, is like the whispers of forever. It's a melody that transcends time, a story that continues to unfold with every passing moment."

As the final chapter of the book unfolded, Ethan and Lily stood in the garden, surrounded by the whispers of forever. The whispers of dawn, though softer now, carried the assurance that in the tapestry of their lives, the garden would forever be a sacred space—a living testament to the enduring power of love, resilience, and the timeless beauty of their shared journey.

ABOUT THE AUTHOR

Derick Chibilu is an upcoming talented author and business professional based in Houston, Texas, where he resides with his beloved wife, Alice, and is known for his inspiring works. Derick holds an MBA from Capella University, a Bachelor of Business in Computer Information Systems from the University of Houston Downtown (UHD), and an Associate of Science in Business Administration from Delaware Tech.

As a born-again Christian, Derick's faith is integral to his life. He is an active member of the North Central Assemblies of God Church in Spring, Texas, where he finds strength and inspiration through fellowship with other believers. Derick strongly believes in God, family, and Christian family values, which are central themes in his writing.

Derick has written extensively on various subjects such as business, leadership, personal development, and Christian spirituality. His works are highly regarded for their clarity, insight, and practicality, making them valuable resources for readers from all backgrounds.

Derick Chibilu's commitment to excellence is evident in everything he does. He is a dedicated professional who takes pride in his work and is constantly seeking new ways to improve himself and his craft. Whether he is writing a new book, delivering a speech, or leading a team, Derick brings passion and enthusiasm to every endeavor.

In summary, Derick Chibilu is an inspiring author and business professional who is making a positive impact on the world. His faith, his family, and his commitment to Christian values deeply influence his life and work. Through his writing, Derick has the power to inspire and uplift readers worldwide.

BOOKS BY MR. DERICK CHIBILU

> **Whimsical Wonders:** 50 Tales of Fictional Fun

> **Love As God Intended It:** Faith, Hope, and Love, But the greatest of these is love.

> **The Bible Storybook**: 50 Exciting Stories for Kids (Volume 1)

> **The Bible Storybook:** 46 Parables: Tales of God's Kingdom and Our Lives (Volume 2)

> **The Bible Storybook**: Exploring The Transformative Power of Faith and The Miraculous Acts of Christ (Volume 3)

> **Shadows of Deception** ~The Hidden Secrets~

> **The Basilica Heist**: Shadows Unveiled

> **Vanishing Chains:** As the intricate plot continues to unfold,

> **Whispers of the Silent Shadows"** Part one

> **Beyond the Veil of Celestial Whispers:** Part Two: The Saga Continues

> **The Prophet Elisha's Unseen Paths**

> **Divine Dwelling:** Unveiling the Mysteries of the Tabernacle

> **Divine Dialogue:** Unveiling the Power of A.C.T.S in the Lord's

Author Contact Information

For information and inquiries or to see other books by the
author:
Email: *Thecblogger4@gmail.com*
Or
Visit Our Website at:
www.booksbyderickchibilu.com

Did you love *Whispers of Dawn" Journey of Healing and Rediscovery*? Then you should read *Whispers of the Silent Shadows : Part one* by DERICK CHIBILU!

In "Whispers of the Silent Shadows," a mysterious disappearance sets the stage for an intricate web of secrets and enigmas. As detective Sarah Reynolds delves into the case, she discovers a series of cryptic messages, hidden rooms, and long-buried family secrets. The story weaves through midnight intrigues, forgotten diaries, and illusions of innocence, keeping readers on the edge of their seats. Can Sarah unravel the tangled threads of deceit before the shadows reveal their haunting truths? Prepare for a suspenseful journey into the heart of a captivating mystery.

Read more at https://www.booksbyderickchibilu.com/.